NEW HORIZONS

science 5~16

KEY STAGE 2

Land, water and air

Jacqueline Dineen

CAMBRIDGE
UNIVERSITY PRESS

Published by the Press Syndicate of the
University of Cambridge
The Pitt Building, Trumpington Street,
Cambridge CB2 1RP
40 West 20th Street, New York,
NY 10011-4211, USA
10 Stamford Road, Oakleigh,
Victoria 3166, Australia

© Cambridge University Press 1992

First published 1992

Designed by Steve Knowlden and Pardoe
Blacker Publishing Ltd, Shawlands Court,
Newchapel Road, Lingfield, Surrey RH7 6BL
Illustrated by Annabelle Brend, Chris Forsey,
Jenny Mumford and Paul Williams

Printed in Great Britain by Scotprint Ltd,
Musselburgh, Scotland.

A catalogue record for this book is available
from the British Library

ISBN 0 521 39755 3

Acknowledgements

The author and publishers would like to thank
the BBC for permission to reproduce the weather
symbols on page 59.

Photographic credits

t=top b=bottom c=centre l=left r=right

Cover: ZEFA

4*l* ZEFA; 6/7*c* S. Nielsen/Bruce Coleman; 8*t* A & J.
Verkaik/ZEFA; 8/9*b* NASA/David Baker; 9*t* Trevor Hill;
10*b* M. Stroud/Planet Earth Pictures; 13*bl* NASA/David
Baker; 13*br* ZEFA; 14*t* Robert Francis/Hutchison
Library; 16*tl* Images; 16*tr* Dr B. Booth/GSF Picture
Library; 16*bl* J. S. Gifford/NHPA; 16*br* Dr B. Booth/GSF
Picture Library; 17*tl* Jon Williams; 17*cl* GSF Picture
Library; 17*tr* David Woodfall/NHPA; 17*cr*, 17*bl*, 17*br*
GSF Picture Library; 18*l* Ken Lucas/Planet Earth
Pictures; 19*t* The Natural History Museum, London;
24*b* Anthony Bannister/NHPA; 26*t* Anthony
Bannister/NHPA; 26*b* Hawaii Natural History
Association/GSF Picture Library; 27*b* ZEFA; 28*t* Jeff
Foott/Bruce Coleman; 28*b* Hälle Flygare/Bruce
Coleman; 31*b* P. McClay/Oxfam; 33*t* Jon Williams;
33*b* ZEFA; 35*t* Peter Scoones/Planet Earth Pictures;
34*b* GSF Picture Library; 36/37*t* Bob Croxford/ZEFA;
40*c* Armstrong/ZEFA; 41*r* Jeff Foott/Bruce Coleman;
43*t* J. Marshall/ZEFA; 43*b* David B. A. Jones/Robert
Harding Picture Library; 48*t* John & Gillian Lythgoe/
Planet Earth Pictures; 48*c* Duncan Murrell/Planet Earth
Pictures; 49*b* Jonathan Chester/NHPA; 51*t* Dr David
Corke/ZEFA; 53*t* Jeremy Hartley/Oxfam; 53*c* Jan
Davis/Oxfam; 57*b* Trevor Hill; 58*l*, 58*tr*, 58*br* The Met.
Office/Crown Copyright; 59*t* University of Dundee;
60*l* Glyn Davies/ICCE; 61*tl* NASA/David Baker.

Contents

Introduction

The Earth is like a ball spinning in space. It is one of the **planets** which **orbit** (travel around) the Sun.

In the beginning, there was no life on Earth. The Earth may have begun as a ball of boiling **molten** rock. It took thousands of millions of years for the Earth to change into the world we know today.

The **climate** has changed a lot. Animals and plants **adapted** to suit the changing world. Some could not adapt, so they died out.

Did you know...?

We think that the first living things were tiny and grew in the seas about 3000 million years ago. All the plants and animals on the Earth today developed from these first living things.

Imagine all the millions of years since the Earth began squashed into one year.

These animals and plants are not drawn to scale. Can you find their real size?

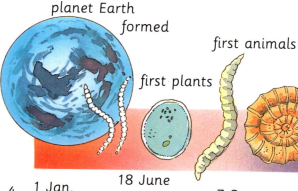

planet Earth formed

first plants

first animals

first **amphibians**

first fish

first trees and **reptiles**

1 Jan.

18 June

7 Sept.

22 Nov.

30 Nov.

4 Dec.

How humans developed

We think that humans may have developed very slowly from ape-like animals which lived in trees. They may have been able to climb down from the trees and run across the ground, like apes today. These animals began to walk on two legs and live on the ground. Over thousands of years, they worked out how to make tools that would help them. Their inventions and discoveries helped the world change more quickly.

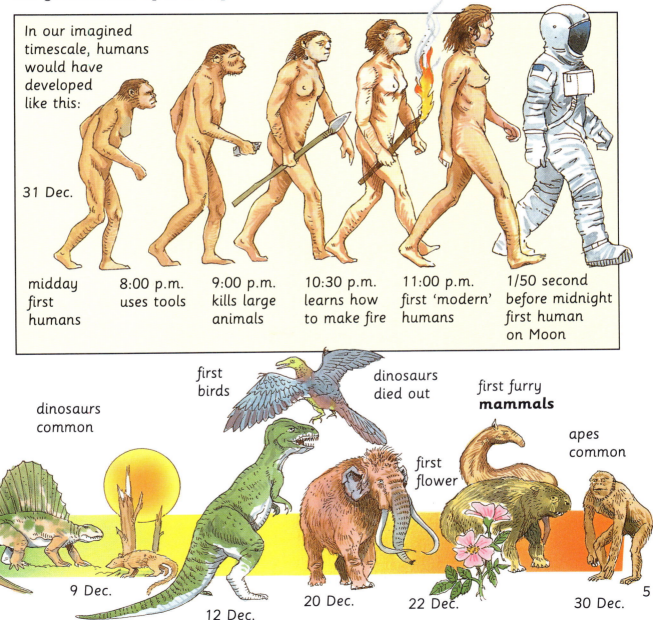

In our imagined timescale, humans would have developed like this:

31 Dec.

midday first humans

8:00 p.m. uses tools

9:00 p.m. kills large animals

10:30 p.m. learns how to make fire

11:00 p.m. first 'modern' humans

1/50 second before midnight first human on Moon

dinosaurs common

first birds

dinosaurs died out

first furry **mammals**

first flower

apes common

9 Dec.

12 Dec.

20 Dec.

22 Dec.

30 Dec.

More about: climate pp10-11 Earth pp14-15 humans pp24-25

5

The Earth in space

If you look at the sky on a clear night, you see lots of stars. The Sun is the closest star. The others are similar to the Sun, but they are much further away. They look like tiny dots in the sky while the Sun looks like a big, fiery ball.

Northern Hemisphere

The solar system

Nine planets orbit the Sun. (There may be others which we do not know about.) They make up the **solar system**. As far as anyone knows, there is no life on the other planets. The amount of sunlight and heat must be right before things will grow. There must be the right sort of land for them to grow on.

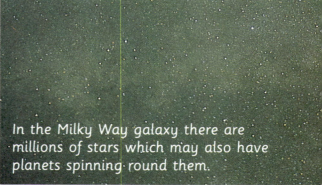
In the Milky Way galaxy there are millions of stars which may also have planets spinning round them.

Jupiter

Mercury

Venus

Sun

Earth

Mars

Saturn

Uranus

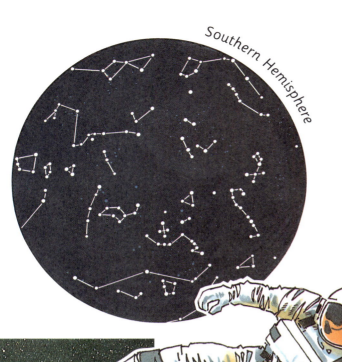

Southern Hemisphere

You can see only the stars which are closest to the Earth. You can see more with a strong telescope, but many stars are too far from Earth to be seen at all.

Gravity

The planets all orbit the Sun. They are held there by the Sun's **gravity**. Gravity is a pull **force**. The Earth's gravity stops everything from floating away into space.

Find out more about the Earth's gravity in the *New Horizons* book, *Energy, forces and communication*.

The nine planets in our solar system are Mercury, Venus, Earth, Mars, Jupiter, Saturn, Uranus, Neptune, and Pluto. They are all different. Can you work out how far each one is from the Sun?

Scale: 1cm = 250 million km

Pluto

Neptune

The planets are not drawn to scale.

Did you know...?

Some of the planets have their own **satellites** or moons. They orbit the planets. The Earth has one satellite, the Moon. Saturn has at least 21 moons circling it!

7

More about: life on Earth pp20-25 the Moon pp12-13 the Sun pp8-11

The Sun

During the day, you can usually see only one star – our Sun. It hides the light of other stars because it is so much closer to the Earth.

On a sunny day we can feel heat from the Sun, although it is 150 million km from the Earth. The Sun is a mass of very hot gases which sends out powerful **rays** of heat and light.

The Sun is always there, even on a cloudy day. Its light rays are powerful enough to shine through cloud and give us daylight.

Measure shadows at different times of the day. Stand a stick or a bottle on the ground in a sunny place. Measure the shadow in the morning, at midday and late in the afternoon. Is the shadow the same length each time? Why?

We need the Sun for life on Earth, but it can harm us, too. Never look straight at the Sun. Its bright light will damage your eyes.

Sunlight and shadows

Rays of light cannot shine through **opaque** objects. If you stand in sunlight, your body stops the rays. It makes a shadow.

The Sun seems to move across the sky all day. When it rises in the morning, it is low in the sky. At midday it is high in the sky. It sets in the evening. It seems to sink down and disappear. In fact, the Sun is not moving. It looks as though it is because the Earth is turning.

Day and night

The Earth orbits the Sun. It also spins round on its own **axis**. You can think of the axis as an invisible rod stretching from the North Pole to the South Pole.

The Earth takes 24 hours to spin right round on its axis.

It is daylight in these parts of the world.

It is night in the parts turned away from the Sun.

As it spins, different parts of the Earth are turned towards the Sun.

More about: clouds pp44-45 Earth's axis pp10-11

Seasons

The Earth is tilted on its axis. As the Earth orbits the Sun, different parts are tilted towards the Sun. That is why we have different **seasons**.

Climates

The countries between the tropics have a **tropical** climate. The Sun's rays are direct and strong. Countries such as Britain are further from the **equator**. They have a **temperate** climate. The Sun's rays are more spread out, so it is always cooler than it is at the equator. It is coldest of all at the North and South Poles.

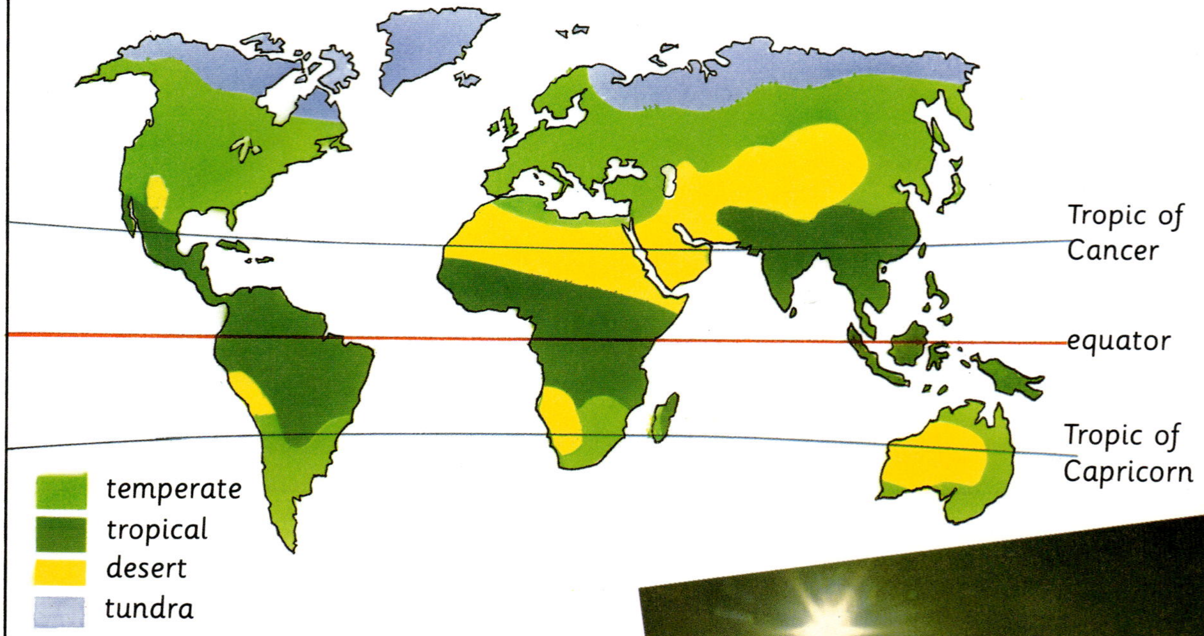

Tropic of Cancer

equator

Tropic of Capricorn

- temperate
- tropical
- desert
- tundra

Find out more about climates in the *New Horizons* book, *Life around us.*

10

The changing seasons

It takes the Earth one year to travel round the Sun.

In June, the North Pole is tilted towards the Sun. It is summer in the northern part of the world and winter in the southern part.

In spring and autumn, the Sun is lower in the sky and its rays spread out more. The days are cooler and shorter.

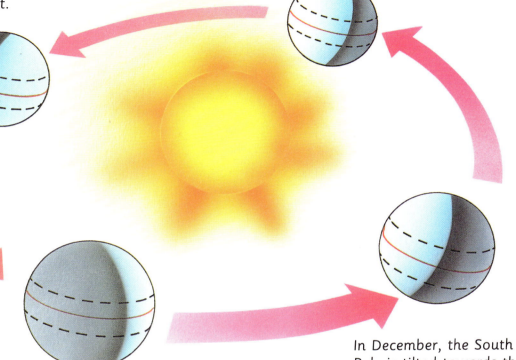

In winter, the Sun is low in the sky. Its rays are slanted instead of shining directly. Even when the Sun is shining brightly, the days feel cold.
During winter near the North or South Pole, there is no daytime at all.

In December, the South Pole is tilted towards the Sun. It is summer in the southern part of the world and winter in the northern part.

Midnight sun at the South Pole

In summer, the Sun is high in the sky. The days are long and hot. During summer near the North or South Pole, there is no night at all.

11

More about: climate pp20-21, 24-25 Sun's rays pp8-9

The Moon

The Moon orbits the Earth. It is held in place by the Earth's gravity. As it moves round, it spins slowly on its axis. It takes nearly one month to orbit the Earth. During that time, it only spins once on its axis.

Phases of the Moon

The Moon looks big and bright in the night sky, but it has no light of its own. What we see is light reflected from the Sun. The Sun shines on only one half of the Moon. During each orbit, different amounts of the sunlit face can be seen from the Earth.

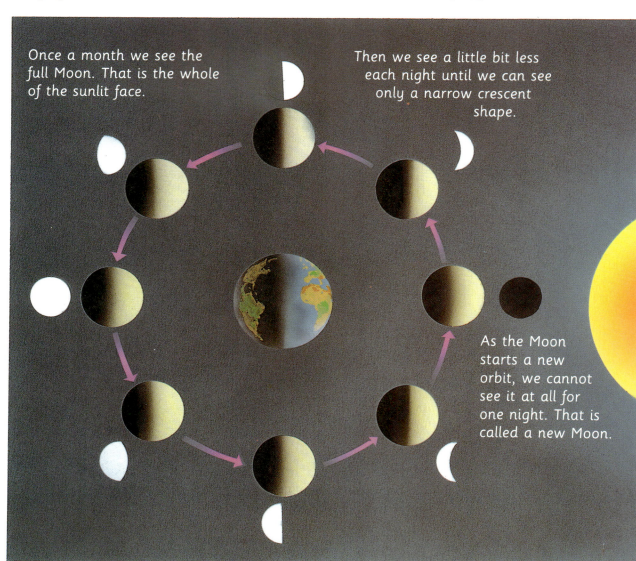

Once a month we see the full Moon. That is the whole of the sunlit face.

Then we see a little bit less each night until we can see only a narrow crescent shape.

As the Moon starts a new orbit, we cannot see it at all for one night. That is called a new Moon.

What is the Moon?

The Moon is much smaller than the Sun. It looks big because it is closer to the Earth.

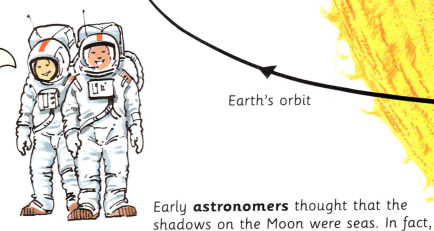

Earth

Moon

Sun

Moon's orbit

Earth's orbit

Did you know...?

The Moon is close enough to the Earth for astronauts to reach it in spacecraft. The first Moon landing was in 1969 when two American astronauts walked on its surface.

The dark side of the Moon

Early **astronomers** thought that the shadows on the Moon were seas. In fact, they are patches of dark rock. The Moon's surface is also covered with round hollows or **craters**, mountains and valleys.

We always see the same face of the Moon from the Earth. In 1959, a spacecraft from the former Soviet Union orbited the Moon. It sent back to Earth the first pictures of the dark side.

What else can you find out about the Moon and Moon landings?

More about: Earth's axis pp9, 10-11 the Moon p37 the Sun pp8-11

What is the Earth?

The Earth is cool and hard on the outside, but inside it is molten rock.

The **crust** is solid rock. It is thicker in some places than in others.

Parts of the **mantle** are so hot that the rock is almost liquid. This sticky, hot rock can move very slowly.

The **core** is extremely hot. It is probably made of two metals, iron and nickel.

crust

mantle

core

The moving crust

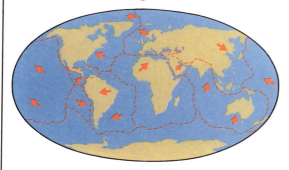

Wherever the plates move together or apart, we find **earthquakes** and **volcanoes**.

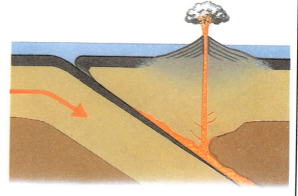

The crust is not a solid shell around the Earth. It is made up of separate pieces, called **plates**, which are dragged about on the moving mantle.

14

> There were no people to draw maps millions of years ago. So how do we know that the land was in different places?

Did you know...?

The Earth's crust is between 35 and 65 km thick under the land, but only about 5 km thick under the seas.

Trace the outlines of the continents from a map of the world on to paper. Cut them out. Can you fit them together?

The story in the rocks

Geologists study the rocks in the crust to see how the Earth has changed. Many scientists believe that the Earth and the Moon were formed at the same time. Some rocks found on the Moon are 4600 million years old, but the oldest rocks found on Earth are about 3800 million years old. Geologists think this is because, as rocks first formed, they were melted again by the heat below.

Fossils of seashells have been found in mountains which are now in the middle of land. This proves that seas once covered those parts of the world.

Geologists can also tell when rocks cracked and folded to form mountains, ridges and valleys. By piecing together all the evidence, they can get a good idea of what the Earth must have looked like at different times.

Look at these maps of the Earth as it was millions of years ago.

The continents move on plates towards or away from each other.

300 million years ago   180 million years ago   65 million years ago

More about: fossils pp18-19, 22   mountains pp28-29   rocks pp16-21

How rocks are formed

There are three types of rock. They are called igneous, sedimentary and metamorphic rock.

Igneous

Igneous rock is formed from **magma**. Magma is molten rock and other material.

Sometimes, the magma forces its way to the surface through a volcano. It cools and hardens in the air to form volcanic rock.

Basalt is a volcanic rock formed on the surface.

Granite is one type of igneous rock which is formed below the surface.

igneous

Sometimes, the magma cools and hardens into rock before it reaches the surface.

metamorphic

Sandstone is formed from grains of sand.

Limestone and sandstone are two sorts of sedimentary rock.

Sedimentary

Sedimentary rock is formed from tiny pieces of rock, sand and mud (sediment) pressed tightly together.

Running water **erodes** (wears away) rocks. Rivers carry tiny pieces of rock into lakes and the sea.

As layers of sediment build up, the layers underneath are pressed more tightly together until they form rock.

sedimentary

Metamorphic

Metamorphic rocks are igneous or sedimentary rocks which have been changed by heat or by being squeezed together under great pressure.

Marble forms when limestone becomes very hot deep in the ground.

Slate forms when soft rock called **shale** is squeezed very tightly.

17

More about: limestone p18   mantle p14   volcanoes pp14, 26-27

The story in fossils

All our evidence about early animals and plants comes from fossils. They can also give us clues about changes in the land and sea.

Chalk is a type of limestone. It is formed from the shells of tiny dead sea animals which have hardened into rock. Sometimes, you can see the fossil prints of animals, plants or shells in the rock.

Find out more about fossils in the *New Horizons* book, *Life around us.*

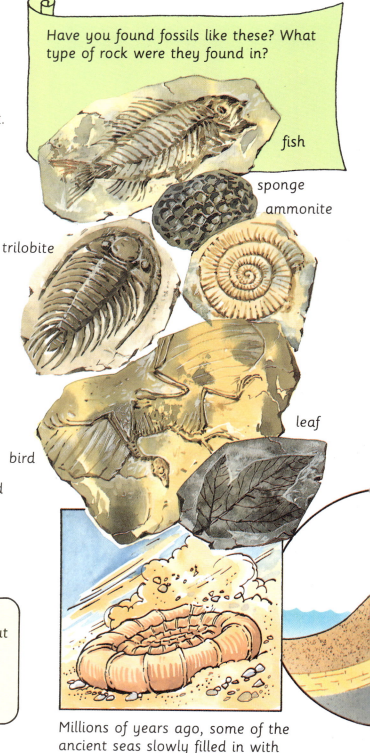

Have you found fossils like these? What type of rock were they found in?

fish

sponge

ammonite

trilobite

bird

leaf

Millions of years ago, some of the ancient seas slowly filled in with sediment.

Metals and precious stones

Rocks are made up of **minerals**. A mineral is any natural substance which is not an animal or a plant. Some minerals contain metals which cooled and hardened in the same way as igneous rocks. Mixtures of minerals and metal are called **ores**. The metal has to be separated from the rock before it can be used.

Metals melt when they are heated and go solid when they are cooled. Most are strong and easy to shape. Gold and silver are precious metals. They are made into expensive objects such as jewellery. Iron and copper are not precious metals.

Diamonds, emeralds, rubies and sapphires are precious stones. They are hard, **transparent** stones which can be cut so that they catch the light and shine brilliantly.

Sometimes, the moving plates squeezed together these new sedimentary rocks. The pressure crushed and folded them . . .

Find out more about metals and how they are used in the *New Horizons* book, *What is it made of?*

. . . so fossils began to appear on the land.

You can even find them near the tops of the highest mountain ranges like the Andes, the Alps or the Himalayas.

19

More about: early animals pp20-25 sedimentary rock pp16-17

Life on Earth

Geologists can tell when animals and plants lived and when they died out by studying the layers of rock they are buried in. The times when changes took place are called geological eras.

Precambrian
(Before 590 million years ago)

Solid rocks began to form on the molten surface about 4500 years ago. The gases given off formed the atmosphere.

Water vapour rising from the hot surface condensed, falling as rain.

Water collected in hollows on the surface, forming seas. Over millions of years, simple plants developed in the seas.

Simple animals such as sponges and jellyfish began to develop. Millions of years later, the seas and lakes were full of life.

Palaeozoic
(590–248 million years ago)

The moving plates of the crust collided and moved apart. Mountains were formed.

The climate was warm and damp.

Forests and swamps covered the land. The first land animals were amphibians. They developed from fish.

Over thousands of years, their fins changed into legs strong enough to carry them across the land.

As the Earth changed, animals and plants changed with it. Some types of animals died out because they could not find food or survive in different climates. Others adapted (changed slowly) to suit differences in the environment.

Mesozoic (248–65 million years ago)	Caenozoic (65 million years ago–present)

Rivers, winds and rain wore away and reshaped the surface of the Earth.

More mountains were formed and eroded giving us the scenery we have today.

Some scientists believe that about 280 million years ago, the weather became hotter and drier. The lakes and swamps dried up and most of the amphibians died out.

The climate became much cooler about 35 million years ago. There were several Ice Ages – the most recent began 2 million years ago.

Reptiles began to develop. They have scaly skins and can survive in a hot, dry climate.

As the climate got warmer again, forests and woodlands grew thicker in areas where ice had melted.

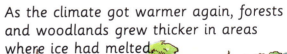

Some reptiles became dinosaurs. Others became mammals. Dinosaurs died out 65 million years ago.

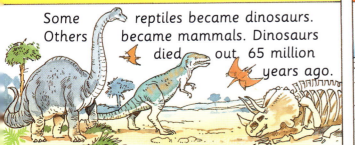

The Ice Age mammals died out or adapted to suit the warmer climate.

21

More about: dinosaurs pp22–23 fossils pp18–19, 22 mammals pp24–25

How we know about dinosaurs

Dinosaurs were a group of reptiles which lived from 200 million years ago until 65 million years ago. No one is quite sure why they died out. It may have been because the weather became colder or hotter. The dinosaurs could not control their body temperature and could not survive great changes in cold or heat.

Scientists have found thousands of dinosaur fossils and pieced them together. You can see whole dinosaur skeletons in some museums.

How do scientists fit the bones together correctly? It has taken many years for scientists to work out what the different dinosaurs looked like.

How many different dinosaurs do you know about? Find out what they ate and how big they were.

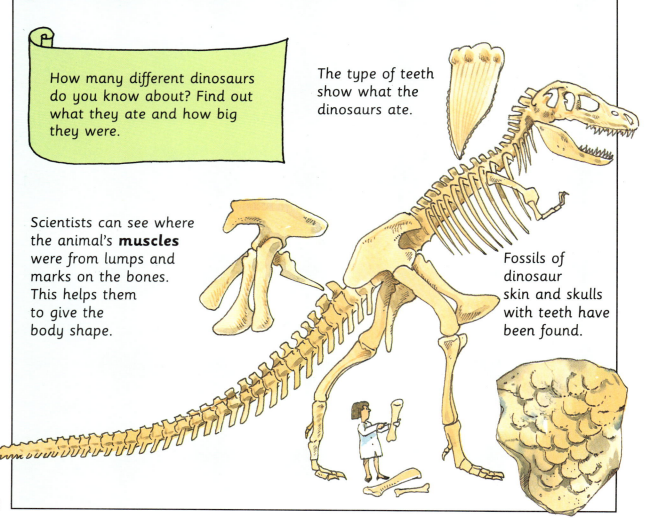

The type of teeth show what the dinosaurs ate.

Scientists can see where the animal's **muscles** were from lumps and marks on the bones. This helps them to give the body shape.

Fossils of dinosaur skin and skulls with teeth have been found.

Find out more about mammals and reptiles in the *New Horizons* book, *Life around us.*

How mammals developed

The first mammals lived about 200 million years ago, at the same time as the dinosaurs. They were small, ate insects and had to hide away from huge meat-eating dinosaurs. They probably came out at night to find food.

When the dinosaurs had died out, the mammals could spread and live in different places. Slowly, they began to change and new types developed.

Some animals lived in trees and ate fruit.

These animals are not drawn to scale.

Others lived on the ground and ate grass and leaves.

The first mammals probably laid eggs. Later, some gave birth to tiny babies. The babies climbed into pouches, like the babies of kangaroos and koala bears.

Some mammals ate meat, catching other animals for food.

More about: dinosaurs p21 fossils pp18-19 mammals pp21, 24-25

Into the last Ice Age

Since the Earth formed there have been at least seven Ice Ages. Parts of the world which now have a temperate climate were covered with ice. They looked like the North and South Poles look today.

Most animals and plants could not live in this icy world. Animals died out or moved into warmer areas. Plants gradually took root in different parts of the Earth.

Cave paintings

We know what people and animals looked like from their bones and fossils. Skeletons have been found in graves dug by Neanderthal people. Stone tools have also been found.

About 40000 years ago, people painted and carved pictures on cave walls. They painted the animals they hunted – woolly mammoths, horses, bison and reindeer.

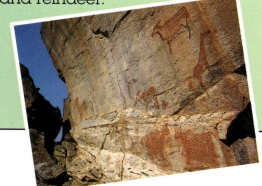

By the start of the last Ice Age, early people were living in Africa. They made simple stone tools and hunted animals for food.

People learned how to plant seeds and farm the land.

Gradually, people spread to other parts of the world. Early human bones were found in China.

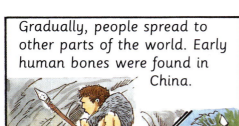

When people discovered fire, they could live in colder parts of the world and adapt to the Ice Age.

Neanderthal people lived in caves, or shelters made from branches and animal skins. They hunted woolly mammoths and cave bears and wore animal skins to keep warm.

About 10 000 years ago, the Earth became warmer. Most of the ice melted. Woolly mammoths and woolly rhinos died out. Plants spread back into the areas where the ice had been.

Did you know...?

The last Ice Age began about two million years ago. It may still be going on because there is always ice and snow in the Arctic and Antarctica. Four million years ago, there was no ice at the Poles. The whole world was warmer than it is now.

Arctic ice today

ice during last Ice Age

25

More about: mammals pp21, 23 humans p5 ice and snow pp48-49

Volcanoes and earthquakes

Volcanoes and earthquakes usually happen near the edges of the Earth's plates.

Magma pushes through the crust. This is called lava.

Lava cools and hardens into rock around the crack.

As the magma builds up again, the pressure forces the plug out.

A crater forms in the top of the volcano.

Magma may burst through in the same place time after time. Over thousands of years, hardened lava builds up around the volcano, forming a mountain. Mount Kilimanjaro in Africa is a volcano. It is over 5000 m high.

Volcanoes

A volcano begins to form when magma escapes through a crack in the Earth's crust.

Volcanoes do not always **erupt** violently. The islands of Hawaii are in the Pacific Ocean. They are all enormous volcanic mountains. The highest, Mauna Kea, rises more than 10 000 m from the sea bed. Today, only Mauna Loa and Kilauea still erupt, but without large explosions.

Earthquakes

Earthquakes can happen where the edges between two plates form huge cracks or **faults**.

The San Andreas fault in California, USA, is over 1000 km long. The edges of the plates are always moving and pushing against each other.
Sometimes, parts of the plates give way and the whole area heaves and shakes.
San Francisco and Los Angeles are always in danger from earthquakes.
A bad earthquake can destroy a whole city. Buildings tumble and thousands of people may be killed.

What else can you find out about volcanoes and earthquakes which have happened recently. Try to find a world map which shows where all the earthquakes and volcanoes in the world happen. Can you explain the pattern they make?

27

More about: crust pp14-15, 28-29   magma pp16, 29   plates pp14-15

Mountains

Mountains are formed by lava and rocks building up around volcanoes. They are also formed by movements of the crust.

Fault-block mountains are formed by faults in the crust. Some rock layers slip down. Others are pushed up like a wall, forming a ridge of mountains. The Teton Mountains in Wyoming, USA, are fault-block mountains. They have flat faces.

The Alps are fold mountains. They stretch for about 1200 km across southern Europe. Mont Blanc in France (4800 m high) and the Matterhorn in Switzerland (4477 m) are in the Alps.

Fold mountains are formed when parts of the crust push against each other. This makes the crust crumple or fold into mountains and valleys.

How old are mountains?

Mountains are always changing. Wind, rain, ice and snow gradually break up the rocks. Rivers and glaciers wear away valleys and remove all the fragments. Sometimes the crust moves again, forming new mountains in the same place. This takes hundreds of millions of years to happen.

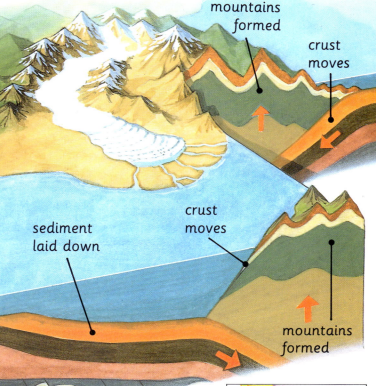

mountains formed

crust moves

sediment laid down

crust moves

mountains formed

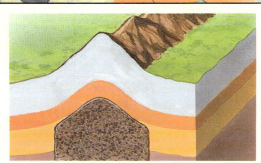

Dome mountains have rounded tops. They are formed when magma forces rock layers to arch up in a dome.

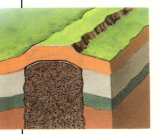

The top of a dome mountain is sometimes worn away to form a **plateau**.

Did you know...?

Tibet

Everest

Nepal   Kanchenjunga

India

Himalaya range

- The world's highest mountain is Mount Everest in the Himalaya range. It is 8848 m high. The third highest, Kanchenjunga (8586 m high) is also in this range.

- The first people to climb to the top of Everest were Edmund Hillary and Tensing Norgay in 1953. In 1975, Junko Tabei from Japan became the first woman to reach the top.

29

More about: erosion pp30-33, 34, 37 volcanoes pp26-27

From rocks to soil

2 Wind and rain gradually broke small pieces of rock away.

1 Thousands of millions of years ago, the Earth's land was just bare rock. There was no soil.

6 When the plants died, they **decayed** and were mixed with the rock pieces. The decayed plants made the soil richer so that more plants could grow. Animals also died and decayed. The decayed plants and animals formed **humus**.

7 Most plants put down roots and need food to grow. Humus helps provide the food for plants.

8 Over millions of years, the soil became richer and richer. It could feed huge forests of trees and plants.

30

3 Wind and water swept the pieces from place to place. They were ground into tiny fragments.

4 In places these small fragments and particles began to build up. This was the start of soil.

Find out more about soil, plants and how they grow in the *New Horizons* book, *Life around us.*

5 Simple plants such as lichen and moss began to grow. They needed only air and water to survive. They could grow in the layer of tiny rock pieces or even on the bare rock itself.

How soil is destroyed

Soil stays useful only if plants grow in it. The roots hold the soil together. When the plants die, they rot into the soil and provide the food new plants need for healthy growth.

In some parts of the world, forests have been cut down. Where nothing has been planted to replace them, rain can wash away the soil. If the soil becomes dry, the wind can blow it away.

31

More about: rain pp46-47, 50-53 wind pp40-41

Rivers

Some rivers begin when underground water comes to the surface as a **spring**.

Rivers start on high ground. Many start in mountains. The start of a river is called the **source**.

When it rains, the water seeps through the soil.

Some rocks have tiny holes.

Water seeps through until it comes to a layer which does not have holes.

Waterfalls are often made when a river flows over hard rock and then soft rock. It wears away the soft rock and leaves a cliff of hard rock.

Tributaries or small streams flow into the main river. It becomes wider.

The water begins to flow sideways. When it reaches the side of a hill or mountain, it trickles out as a spring.

Did you know...?

The longest river in the world is the Nile in Egypt (6669 km long). The Amazon in South America is not quite as long, but it is wider. The mouth of the Amazon is 333 km wide.

The land slopes more gently at the bottom of the mountain. The river flows more slowly. It winds through the hills in a much broader valley.

Near the sea, the land is often flatter. The river **meanders** in S-bends.

Sometimes silt builds up at the mouth of the river. The river cuts channels through it. This is called a **delta**.

When the water rushes down
the steep mountainside,
it carries soil and stones with it.
The fast-flowing water cuts a
deep V-shaped valley.

The Grand Canyon in the USA was carved out by the Colorado river. It has taken nearly 10 million years. The canyon is 1·6 km deep and nearly 30 km wide in places.

The water flows more quickly
on the outside of the bend.
It wears away the bank.

The water flows slowly on the
inside. It drops soil and stones.
The bends become tighter.

Not all rivers flow out to the sea. Some flow into lakes. Some flow into the desert and disappear into the sand.

The river is still carrying soil when it reaches the sea. Most rivers flow straight out into the sea and this **silt** is washed away.

Suez canal

Cairo

Nile delta

A satellite view of the Nile delta in Egypt.

Did you know...?
The highest waterfalls in the world are the Angel Falls in Venezuela, South America (979 m high). The widest are the Khone Falls on the Mekong river in Laos (108 km wide).

33

More about: lakes pp34-35 mountains pp26, 28-29 sea pp36-37

Lakes

A lake is formed when a hollow is filled with water. The water comes from rivers, streams and the rain. Lakes must be topped up all the time to stop them drying up.

Many lakes began during the last Ice Age.

Huge **glaciers** moving down mountainsides, carved out U-shaped valleys and hollows in the rocks.

When the weather got warmer, the glaciers began to melt and turned into rivers. The hollows filled with water forming small lakes called tarns.

Did you know...?

The Great Lakes in North America are linked together to form the biggest stretch of fresh water in the world. Lake Superior is the largest lake in the world (82 350 km^2).

Canada
Superior
Huron
Michigan
Ontario
Erie
USA

Sometimes, rocks carried by the ice were dropped across the valleys like huge dams. Rivers could not flow past and spread out to form lakes

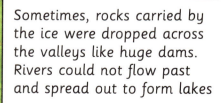

Other sorts of lake

In the Great Rift Valley in Africa, two faults run side by side. The land in between has sunk to form a long, wide valley.

In places, the land has sunk further. Water filled the hollows to form large lakes along the valley.

Lake Tanganyika

Lake Malawi

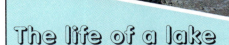

The life of a lake

Most lakes do not last forever. Rivers and streams carry sediment into the lakes. The lakes slowly fill up until they disappear completely. The Dead Sea has the saltiest water on Earth. The Jordan river deposits salty sediments in the lake. These build up as the water evaporates.

North of the Great Rift Valley lakes is Lake Victoria. When the crust buckled, the shallow basin filled with water.

Some lakes form in the craters of volcanoes which have stopped erupting.

Can you find out what animals live in lakes or round their banks?

35

More about: glaciers p29 rivers pp32-33 sediment pp17, 29, 32-33

The sea

Rivers and lakes usually contain fresh water. When the seas first formed, the water was fresh. As rocks on land were worn away by the weather, mineral salts were released from them. Rivers carried the salts to the sea. Over millions of years, the water became the salty mixture of today.

Waves

Waves are caused by the wind blowing over the sea. There is always some wind, even if you cannot feel it much. Waves can be made by storms hundreds of kilometres away. They grow as they travel across the sea.

Did you know...?

Most waves are less than 3 m high. The highest ever seen (37 m high) was in the Pacific Ocean in 1933.

Some currents are very strong. Swimmers can be swept away by them.

Currents

Sea water moves around in **currents**, caused mostly by the movement of cold and warm water. Cold water sinks under warmer water. It flows towards the equator. There it is warmed up and rises. Then it flows back towards the north and south.

The power of the sea

The sea pounds against rocks and cliffs, slowly wearing them away. Sandstone is broken down into grains of sand. Harder stone is worn into smooth pebbles. Waves carve away the cliffs. Sometimes, buildings near the edge fall into the sea.

Tides

Tides are caused by the pull of gravity from the Moon.

pull makes the sea deeper

low tide

Moon moves around the Earth

sea

Earth

as effect of pull passes, tide goes out

high tide

HIGH

LOW

This map shows the main ocean currents

warm
cold

More about: mineral salts p35 Moon pp12-13 sandstone p17

What is the weather?

(km)

900

800

'Weather' means the condition of the atmosphere over a short time. 'Climate' means the usual conditions found in a particular area from season to season.

In temperate climates such as Britain, there are many changes in the weather. There may be sunshine, rain, snow, hail, fog or wind. Nearer the equator, the weather does not vary much.

Why does the weather change?

700

600

As the Earth developed over hundreds of millions of years, gases rose up from it. They massed together and formed an envelope of air around the Earth. This is the **atmosphere**.

The atmosphere is made up from these gases.

500

400

The atmosphere is nearly 500 km thick. It presses down on the Earth. The air at the bottom is squeezed down more tightly than the air at the top. This is called the air **pressure**. Changes in the air pressure at the bottom of the atmosphere give us changes in the weather.

carbon dioxide

oxygen

nitrogen

water vapour and other gases

300

200

100

50

Water **vapour** cools to form huge white clouds of tiny water droplets.

sea level

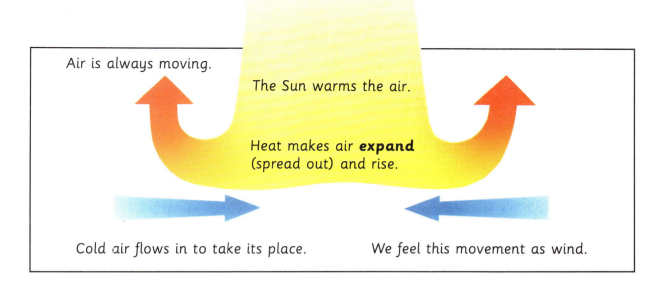

Air is always moving.

The Sun warms the air.

Heat makes air **expand** (spread out) and rise.

Cold air flows in to take its place.

We feel this movement as wind.

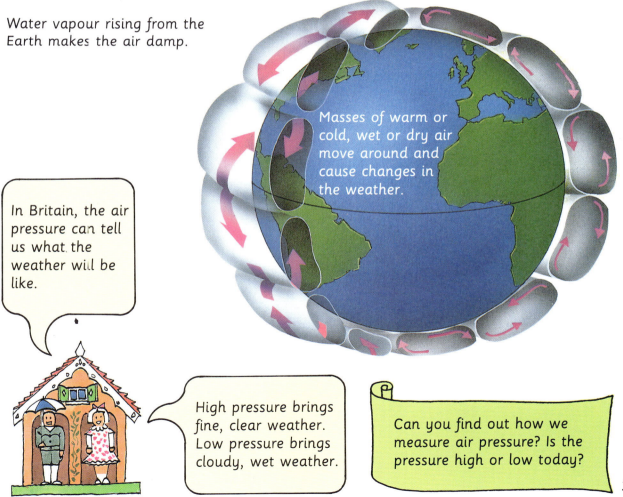

Water vapour rising from the Earth makes the air damp.

Masses of warm or cold, wet or dry air move around and cause changes in the weather.

In Britain, the air pressure can tell us what the weather will be like.

High pressure brings fine, clear weather. Low pressure brings cloudy, wet weather.

Can you find out how we measure air pressure? Is the pressure high or low today?

39

More about: climate pp10-11 clouds pp44-46 water vapour pp42-51

The wind

The wind can be gentle or strong. It can blow from any direction, whatever the season. The Sun warms the air and keeps it moving. Other things affect the direction and strength of the wind.

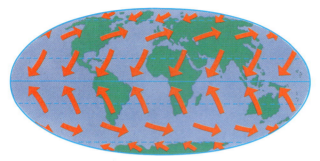

There is a pattern of world winds. Some winds always blow in the same direction. The trade winds always blow towards the equator. The air at the equator is hot. It rises and streams of colder air blow in to take its place.

Changing direction

During the day, air over the land warms up more quickly than air over the sea.

It rises and colder air blows in from the sea.

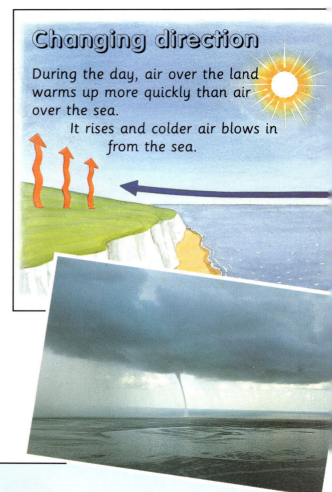

Hurricanes and tornadoes

A hurricane is a tropical storm with very strong winds and heavy rain. The wind is so strong that it can uproot trees and blow the roofs off buildings. Hurricanes build up over the seas in the tropics. Warm, damp air rises quickly and towering clouds develop. Strong damp winds blow in and start to circle round as they move upwards.

A tornado is also a swirling spiral of air. It is smaller, faster and builds up over the land. It is a whirlwind which can blow down buildings.

In 1987, a hurricane hit Britain. Hundreds of trees were uprooted and many buildings were damaged.

Typhoons are hurricanes which start in the China Sea and the western Pacific Ocean. Hong Kong has typhoons every year.

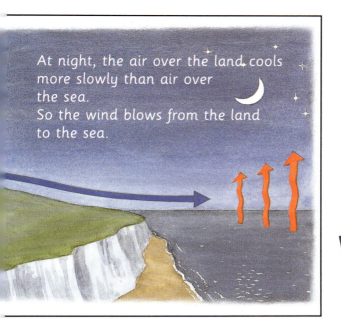

At night, the air over the land cools more slowly than air over the sea.
So the wind blows from the land to the sea.

Did you know...?
Dust on Barbados in the Caribbean contains minerals from Europe and Africa on the other side of the Atlantic Ocean.

The wind can blow on and on if there is nothing to stop it, but it cannot blow through solid objects. High mountains can force the wind to change direction.

Strong, hot desert winds blow up sand and dust. They can carve strange shapes from the rocks.

The wind is named after the direction it is blowing from. So a north wind is blowing from the north to the south.

Did you know...?
Sometimes the wind blows at 800 km/h. A straw blown by a tornado can stick into a tree-trunk.

41

More about: rain pp44-47, 50-53 sea pp36-37 tropics pp10, 51-53

When the air cools

If you watch water boil, you can see what heat does to water.

The heat makes the water **evaporate** or turn into water vapour.

As the water boils, you can see clouds of tiny water droplets.

It is hot and the droplets soon become invisible, dry water vapour.

When the air hits a cold surface, it cools down.

The water vapour **condenses** or turns back into drops of water.

Dew

If you go out before the Sun has warmed the air, you will see that everything is often covered with drops of water, even though it has not been raining. This water is called dew.

Water evaporates during the day. At night, the air cools. The water vapour in the air condenses into droplets on the ground. When the Sun begins to shine, the dew evaporates. There is more dew after a hot day because more water can evaporate.

Frost is frozen dew. It makes patterns on window panes. Frost starts to melt as soon as the Sun begins to shine.

Mist and fog

Mist and fog are clouds which form close to the ground. In the early morning when the air is still and cool, the air is heavy with water vapour which condenses into mist.

Fog is formed in the same way, but it is thicker. Very damp air condenses into a thick blanket of cloud. If the Sun cannot shine through it to make the water evaporate, the fog can last all day.

Sometimes, fog is so thick that you can hardly see anything. It is very dangerous for drivers.

The thickest mists form over areas where there is water such as the sea, lakes, rivers, and marshes. When the Sun shines, the water evaporates and the mist disappears.

In places like downland where there are no rivers or streams, you may see round ponds lined with stone. They are called dewponds. Farmers build them to collect the dew for animals to drink.

In the desert, days are very hot and nights are very cold so dew forms. Sometimes, it is the only water for months on end.

43

More about: clouds pp44-45, 50-51 water cycle pp46-47

What clouds tell us

You can tell a lot about the weather from the shape of the clouds and how high in the sky they are. Clouds do not stay still. The wind blows them across the sky. Sometimes, clouds appear in a bright blue sky. They mass together and it rains. At other times, the day starts cloudy and the wind blows the clouds away. The weather becomes brighter.

Altostratus are rain clouds which look like a grey sheet.

There is a saying 'mackerel sky, not long dry' because these clouds are usually the first sign that rain clouds are coming.

Cirrus clouds are often called mare's tails because they look like streaming horse's tails in the sky.

Cumulonimbus clouds are tall, thick and bring heavy rain, often with thunder and lightning.

nimbostratus

Cirrus clouds form so high that the water in them turns to drops of ice.

cirrostratus

cirrocumulus

Altocumulus clouds are small and round. This is often called a mackerel sky because the clouds look like the pattern on the fish.

cumulus

stratus

stratocumulus

Fog forms at ground level when it is cold and there is little or no wind.

More about: condensation pp42-43, 46 fog p43 rain pp46-47

Why it rains

The Sun shines on seas, rivers and lakes. Its heat makes some of the water evaporate.

Higher up, the air is colder. The water vapour condenses into tiny drops of water which mass together to form clouds.

The droplets grow and become heavy. They fall as rain.

Winds blow it to the land.

Water vapour rises into the air from the sea.

This movement of water is called the water cycle. It never stops.

Sometimes the wind blows air into the side of a mountain.

The wind blows on, but it has no vapour in it now.

It is dry on the other side of the mountain. This is called a rain shadow area.

Rain falls on one side of the mountain.

Rain fills up the rivers and lakes that drain into the seas.

47

More about: clouds pp44-45 evaporation pp42-43 rain pp50-53

Ice and snow

Ice is solid water. When the weather is very cold, a layer of ice forms on ponds and lakes.

Snow is formed in clouds which rise high in the sky. The air there is freezing. When the water drops in the clouds freeze, they fall as snowflakes.

When snow is pressed down under people's feet it becomes compressed or solid. It turns into ice.

A glacier can move slowly downhill. It carries rocks and stones which gouge out U-shaped valleys.

Snow lies on the ground in a thick, soft blanket until the Sun's heat melts it. When you walk in it, your feet sink in.

Glaciers are made from compressed snow. Layers of snow pile up in high mountains. The lower layers are pressed down so tightly that they turn into ice.

On freezing winter nights, rainwater on the roads turns to ice. The ice is slippery and dangerous for drivers.

Snow has to be cleared from roads because cars cannot drive through thick snow.

Icebergs

Icebergs are floating mountains of ice in the oceans around Antarctica and the Arctic. They are formed when huge glaciers push their way to the sea. The end of the glacier breaks off to form an iceberg.

Hail

In thunder clouds, drops of water move upwards.

Cold air freezes the water and the drops grow bigger.

Strong upward currents of air can keep large hailstones in the air for several hours.

Sleet

Sometimes, rain falls when there is a cold wind.

The raindrops pass through a freezing layer of air.

They freeze into drops of ice which usually melt when they hit the ground.

Hailstones can do a lot of damage. They can dent cars and batter buildings. During summer thunderstorms, they can flatten whole fields of crops.

Did you know...?

Some hailstones are as big as tennis balls! One of the biggest hailstones in the world weighed 750 g.

49

More about: clouds pp44-45 glaciers p29 thunderstorms pp50-51

Storms

Storms build up when the air is hot and damp or **humid**. Water vapour rises quickly and the air feels 'heavy'. Large masses of cloud form which are full of rain. Before the storm, currents of cold air rush down and meet warm air rising from the Earth. **Torrential** rain begins to fall. Lightning flashes across the sky and there are loud claps of thunder.

Lightning is caused by **electricity** in the atmosphere.

Hot and cold air churn around in the thunderclouds.

A strong electric charge builds up. When the charge becomes powerful enough, a huge electric spark jumps to the Earth or to other clouds.

This is a flash of lightning.

When it is hot and humid, people often say that there is a storm on the way.

A streak of lightning heats up the air and makes it expand so quickly that it causes a loud bang. This is thunder.

Monsoons

A monsoon is a wind which brings months of rain to parts of the tropics. All through summer, the land is very hot. Warm, damp winds blow in from the seas. The air rises and forms clouds. Torrential rain falls. This is called the rainy season.

In winter, the land cools down. Cool, dry winds blow from the land to the sea. The weather is dry for months.

51

More about: rain pp46-47, 52-53 storm clouds p44 wind pp39-41, 44

Floods and droughts

Floods

Sometimes, when it rains a lot, or
snow melts quickly, there are floods.
Rivers become very full and burst
their banks.

The Netherlands is a flat country.
In parts of the Netherlands, the land
is below sea level. There are often
floods.

The Dutch people have built strong walls
called **dykes** to hold back flood water.

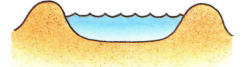

Floods can also be held back if the banks
of rivers are built up so that they are
higher than the flood level.

At one time, windmills pumped water
from the land into channels called
canals. Now diesel pumps are used.

The mouth of the Ganges river in Bangladesh is the largest delta in the world. The land is flat and there are often floods during the rainy season. Many people lose their homes and their crops.

Droughts

Sometimes, when it does not rain for weeks, there is a **drought**. In Britain, people are told not to use too much water. They cannot water their gardens or wash their cars.

In countries where there is one rainy season a year, a drought can be very serious such as in Ethiopia in Africa. There is no water for the crops or for animals to drink. Many people may die of starvation.

In California, USA, the drought is less serious. People can afford to buy water from other places.

During a long drought, the ground becomes hard and cracks. When it does rain, the water cannot soak into the ground. It runs away and is wasted. Often, heavy rain washes away the soil.

shaduf

canals

well

People in some countries have ways of controlling water so they can grow crops. This is called **irrigation**.

53

More about: rain pp44, 46-47 snow pp48-49 water pp32-36

Studying the weather

Hurricanes, storms, floods and droughts can ruin people's lives. If people have some warning about them, they may be able to protect themselves and their homes.

People who study the weather are called **meteorologists**. They give weather **forecasts** which tell people what the weather should be like for the next day or two.

Meteorologists can sometimes tell which way a hurricane will come and warn people. They can forecast rainfall and try to give flood or drought warnings.

Farmers rely on knowing how the weather will affect their crops. Crops need sunshine to ripen. Rain can ruin them. Farmers have to harvest the crops when the weather is dry.

Meteorologists study the build-up of clouds, wind direction and changes of air pressure. They have equipment to help them, but forecasting is not easy. Conditions can change quickly.

Sailors and fishers need to know what the weather will be like at sea. Storms make the sea rough and dangerous. Blankets of fog can come down suddenly.

In Britain, the weather changes a lot. It can be hot and sunny one day and pouring with rain the next. That is why people talk about the weather so much!

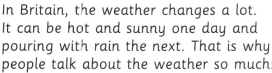

If you are planning a picnic, you want to know if it will rain.

If you are going sailing, you want to know how strong the wind will be.

Reading the signs

Red sky at night, shepherd's delight.
Red sky in the morning, shepherd's warning.

Have you heard this saying? It means that if the sky looks red in the evening, the next day will be fine. If it is red in the morning, the weather will turn bad. Do you think this saying is true?

Can you find out about any other sayings? The pictures give clues. Do you think they are true?

55

More about: fog pp43, 45 sea pp36-37 weather forecast pp57-59

Collecting the information

Meteorologists have to measure weather conditions every few hours. Instruments record changes in the atmosphere such as wind, clouds and air pressure. Information is exchanged with meteorologists in other countries.

There are weather stations all over the world. Some are on land . . .

Wind speeds and other conditions change in different layers of air, so meteorologists send up balloons filled with gas. Instruments on the balloons measure wind speed and direction, air pressure, temperature and humidity at different heights. A radio is attached which sends the information back to the weather station.

These stations measure the temperature, the air pressure, the strength of the wind, amount of rainfall, and sunshine.

. . . others are on ships at sea.

Satellites circle the Earth and automatic cameras take pictures of the atmosphere. These pictures show where clouds are and how they are moving.

Aircraft carry instruments which take weather measurements.

All the information is collected at central weather stations where meteorologists plot a weather forecast.

That is why we talk about temperature as 'degrees in the shade'.

Measuring the temperature

The temperature of the air is measured using a **thermometer**. If a thermometer is left outside in direct sunlight, it will show a higher temperature than the air around it. Special screens, called Stevenson screens, shade thermometers from the Sun's rays.

57

More about: clouds pp44-46 weather forecast pp54, 58-59 wind pp39-41

The weather forecast

At a central weather station, information pours in from all directions. Thousands of measurements and observations come in each day. Now they have to be turned into an accurate weather forecast for each part of the country.

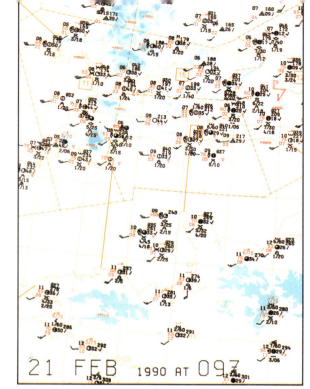

21 FEB 1990 AT 09Z

The computer works out wind speeds, rainfall and temperature for different points on a map, called 'gridpoints'. Conditions change higher up in the atmosphere, so the computer makes calculations for several different levels above each gridpoint.

The information is fed into a computer. Sometimes, an instrument may not be working properly. Meteorologists have to try to spot any errors so that the forecast will be accurate.

Using these calculations, the computer works out how the weather will change later in the day. It can also work out the weather for up to a week later.

Did you know...?
More than 2 million weather forecasts are issued in Britain every year.

Presenting the weather forecast

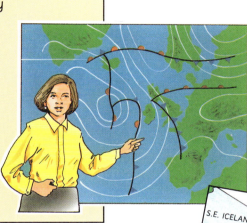

The weather forecast is passed to radio and television stations. The 'weather men and women' on television are usually meteorologists, too. They use maps which the viewers can understand.

The maps show areas of high and low pressure and the directions they are moving in. The forecasters explain what sort of weather this will bring. They also show satellite pictures of cloud cover.

Meteorologists compare the computer calculations with other evidence such as photographs from satellites. They make sure that both show the same things happening. If there are differences, they work out why and correct the computer's calculations.

What do these television weather symbols mean?

The shipping forecast

The weather forecast warns a ship's crew of wind, storms and fog. They can alter their route to avoid the bad weather, or protect their cargo from damage.

The shipping forecast advises the best route to take. It describes the wind, waves and visibility in different sea areas. Sometimes it is better to take a longer route to avoid bad weather. Strong winds and high waves can slow ships down and cause damage.

59

More about: measuring the weather pp56–57 sea pp36–37

Changes in the atmosphere

Today, the Earth is crowded with people and machines. We may be changing the atmosphere.

The greenhouse effect

The glass in a greenhouse lets in the Sun's heat and traps it. Earth's atmosphere acts like a greenhouse. The right amount of heat is trapped by the gases, so the Earth is not too hot or too cold.

CFC gases used in some aerosol sprays and refrigerators may harm the atmosphere.

One of the gases in the atmosphere is **carbon dioxide**. It is given off by burning fuels such as coal and oil. Today more and more fuels are being burned, producing more and more carbon dioxide.

Plants use carbon dioxide and water to make food and oxygen. As people chop down huge areas of rain forest, less carbon dioxide is absorbed. Some scientists believe that as more carbon dioxide builds up in the atmosphere, the Earth will get warmer. This is known as 'global warming'.

Global warming could have dangerous side effects. If all the ice in the polar regions melts, sea levels will rise. Many areas of the world will be flooded.

This satellite picture, above, shows the 'hole' in the ozone layer above the South Pole in 1985.

The ozone layer

The Earth is protected from the Sun's dangerous rays by a layer of gas in the atmosphere called ozone. The ozone layer is between 20 and 50 km above the Earth's surface. Some gases produced on Earth are making the ozone layer thinner, especially over the North and South Poles.

Many people are worried about Earth's future. Some countries are trying to control the burning of fuels and warn about cutting down the rain forests. They persuade people to use CFC-free aerosols. We all must learn how to protect our planet.

This is how Earth might look millions of years in the future. If our atmosphere is destroyed, all of the water would evaporate. It could not be replaced.

More about: atmosphere p38 water cycle pp46-47

Key words

The meanings of words can depend on how and when they are used. You may find that as you learn more about science the meanings change slightly.

adapt to change to suit different surroundings

amphibian an animal such as a frog or a toad, which is born in water, but lives as an adult mostly on dry land

astronomer a person who studies the stars and planets

atmosphere the layer of gases which surrounds the Earth

axis an imaginary straight line around which something turns

canal a water channel built to join two areas of water, or to carry flood water away from the land

carbon dioxide one of the gases in air

climate the usual weather conditions of an area or country

condense to turn back from gas to liquid: for example, from water vapour to water droplets

core the centre of the Earth

crater a deep bowl-shaped hollow in the ground

crust the rocky, outer layer of the Earth

current flowing streams in the sea

decay to rot

delta fan-shaped area of land at the mouth of a river formed from sediment dropped by the river. The river divides into channels as it flows through the silt

drought a long dry period

dyke a long, strong wall built to hold back flood water

earthquake sudden shaking of the Earth's crust caused by movement along a fault or volcanic activity beneath the surface

electricity a way of moving energy using electric charges

equator the imaginary line around the middle of the Earth

erode to wear away by moving water, wind or ice

erupt to burst out

evaporate to turn liquid into a gas: for example, water turns into water vapour when heated

expand to get bigger

fault a crack in the rock layers in the Earth's crust

force a push or a pull. Forces can start or stop an object moving or change its shape

forecast statement of what will probably happen later

fossil a print or the remains of an animal or plant, found in rock

geologist a scientist who studies the rocks on and under the surface of the Earth

glacier a large body of slow-moving ice in a valley

gravity the pull on all objects due to the Earth

humid moist, damp

humus decayed animals and plants which are part of the soil

irrigate to water land and crops using artificial channels and pipes. Water comes from deep wells, rivers or dams. Irrigation makes it possible to grow crops in dry places

magma molten rock from beneath the Earth's crust

mammal an animal covered with hair which has a backbone; most give birth to live young and produce milk to feed them. Its body temperature stays the same

mantle part of the Earth between the crust and the core

meander to follow a winding course; swing from side to side

meteorologist a scientist who studies the atmosphere and weather

mineral any natural substance found in the ground which has not been formed from plants or animals. Rocks and metals are minerals

molten melted, made liquid

muscles your muscles pull your bones to make them move

opaque something which you cannot see through

orbit the path of a planet or satellite as it moves around another body

ore rock and soil which contains useful substances, such as metal

plate the huge sections of the Earth's crust

plateau the flat, level top which some mountains have

planet any one of the bodies in space, including Earth, in orbit around the Sun

pressure pushing or pressing down on a substance

rays beams of light from the Sun

reptile an animal which cannot control the temperature of its body. It becomes hot when the temperature around it is hot and cold when the temperature is cold

satellite a natural or artificial object which orbits a planet, such as a moon or weather satellite

season one of the main periods in a year. In temperate climates, there are four seasons, spring, summer, autumn and winter. In tropical areas, there is a rainy season and a dry season

shale sedimentary rock produced from clay

silt the mud and sand carried along by a river

solar system the Sun and the planets which go round it

source a thing or place from which something comes: the place from which a stream or river starts

spring a place where underground water comes to the surface

temperate describes a climate which has warm summers and cool winters

thermometer an instrument for measuring temperature

torrential very heavy downpour of rain

transparent letting light through so that objects can be clearly seen

tropical describes the climate near the equator. The area around the tropics

vapour the gas which a liquid turns into when it evaporates

volcano a place where boiling, molten rock reaches the Earth's surface

Index